250
ANIMAL ANSWERS

Published by Lowe & B. Hould, a division of Borders Group, Inc.
100 Phoenix Drive, Ann Arbor, MI 48108, USA

Lowe & B. Hould is a trademark of Borders Properties, Inc.

Devised and produced by
Tucker Slingsby Ltd,
Berkeley House,
73 Upper Richmond Road,
London SW15 2SZ

Designed by Helen James
Cover design by Peter Bennett

Printed and bound in Italy by Garzanti Verga

ISBN 1-902272-08-0

250
ANIMAL ANSWERS

Steve Parker

Illustrated by Graham Rosewarne

Lowe & B. Hould

About this book

There are animals everywhere: flying in the sky, burrowing under the earth, swimming in the oceans, running through the forest, and even sharing your home. Every day you will see lots of different animals. In a town you may spot cats, dogs, birds, and plenty of bugs. If you live in the country, there will be farm animals, pets, and wild creatures to watch. In addition to the animals alive today, there are many that you can now see only as drawings in books or models in museums. These are the creatures, such as dinosaurs, that no longer survive on Earth.

I have always been fascinated by animals and have studied how they behave and written many books about them. Over the years, lots of children have asked me questions about animals – ranging from "Do animals go to school?" to "Why don't dinosaurs still roam the Earth?" Packed into these pages are the answers I've discovered to lots and lots of children's questions about animals and how they live. So if you want to be an animal expert, just keep turning these pages. They are full of fascinating facts!

Steve Parker

Contents

Have houses?

Many animals do live in houses, but they are not built of brick or lumber with glass windows like the house you probably live in. Animal houses are usually made of wood, mud or stones. They shelter animals from bad weather and from enemies. Animals can rest, eat, and store food there. They often raise a family inside, too. Some animals build a new home each year. Others keep the same home for most of their lives.

Look into a pond in summer. You may see what look like stones crawling along the bottom. This is the tube-shaped house of a **caddisfly larva**, the young of the caddisfly. These larvae make their homes from leaves, sticks, or pebbles, which they glue together with a slimy liquid. The head and legs of the caddisfly larva poke out at one end.

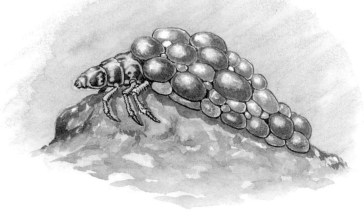

Eagles have very spacious homes. They build the biggest nests of any bird, perching them high on a cliff ledge or in a tall tree. The nests, called eyries, are huge piles of sticks and twigs. A mother and father eagle may have several eyries. Each year they choose one to live in, then add more twigs to make it bigger and stronger. Some eyries are as large as a small car!

Before **beavers** can build their house, called a lodge, they must make a lake to put it in. First they build a dam in a stream. This stops the water flowing past and slowly creates a large lake. The beavers can then build their lodge. This is a strong pile of twigs, branches, mud, and stones. It has underwater entrances and living and sleeping chambers. Enemies, such as wolves, cannot get in. This picture shows you what it is like inside a lodge.

A **snail** not only lives in a house, it takes its house wherever it goes. This house is its shell. As the animal grows, so the shell grows too. The snail can pull itself inside its shell and seal up the doorway. This keeps out enemies and helps it to stay cool and moist in hot weather.

9

Change shape?

As bugs grow up, their bodies change. This means that they can do different things at each stage of their lives. Insects start as tiny eggs. But a hard-shelled egg cannot eat, so the eggs then hatch into a second stage, the larva. The larva is an eating machine and this is the main feeding stage. Some larvae, such as butterfly caterpillars, look very different from the adults. They will change shape again to become full-grown adults. Other types of larvae, such as insect nymphs and baby spiders, look like their parents. They only change their shape slightly. They grow bigger until they, too, become adults.

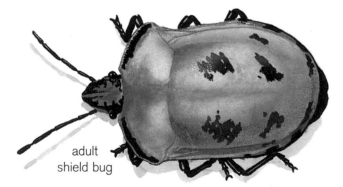

adult
shield bug

A **shield bug** has a strong, hard body casing, like a knight-in-armor's shield. The newly hatched young are called nymphs. They are similar to the parents, but their bodies are a slightly different shape and have no wings. They feed, grow and molt, or shed their skins, several times. Each time they molt, they look more like the adult.

Maggots squirm and writhe as they feed on moldy meat. Soon they will fly away. But how, without wings? Maggots and similar grubs are the larvae of flies such as the **greenbottle**. The soft-skinned larvae eat, molt, wriggle, eat, molt and so on. Then they change into tough-cased pupae. Inside the case, the fly forms its adult body. Finally it emerges and buzzes off!

shield bug nymphs

10

These pictures show each stage in the life of an insect called a **swallowtail butterfly**. It begins as an egg. This hatches into the young form, or larva. In butterflies and moths, we call this a caterpillar. The larva molts several times as it grows. Then it becomes a hard-cased pupa, or chrysalis in the case of butterflies and moths. Inside the chrysalis, the body parts move around and change shape.

Egg

Young caterpillar
(larva)

Older caterpillar
(larva)

At last the adult emerges, crumpled and damp, from the chrysalis. The butterfly spreads its wings to dry, and then flits off to find a partner. This complete change in body shape is called metamorphosis. Other insects that go through these four different stages are moths, beetles, flies, bees, wasps, and ants. Most other insects change shape gradually, from nymphs into the adults. This group includes shield bugs, grasshoppers, crickets, dragonflies, and mayflies.

Adult butterfly

Chrysalis (pupa)

11

Need air?

Not exactly. Animals need oxygen. This is an invisible gas. It's needed to make your body work. Oxygen helps to free the energy in the food that you have eaten and digested. All animals must have this energy to live, grow, and move about. Oxygen makes up one-fifth of the air around us. Land animals get oxygen by breathing air into their lungs or similar body parts. Oxygen is also found in water. The fresh water of streams, ponds, rivers, and lakes, and the salt water of seas and oceans contain oxygen. Water animals can take in this oxygen through their gills or similar body parts.

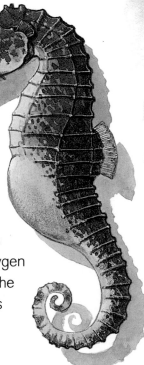

The **seahorse** does not look like an ordinary fish. It has a horse-shaped head and a curly tail to grip seaweed or rocks. But like all fish, it has gills for breathing under the water. The gills are just behind the eyes. Water comes in through the mouth and flows over the gills. The gills take oxygen from the water into the body. The water flows out through gill slits on the sides of the head.

Dolphins live in water, but they cannot stay under for ever. This is because they are not fish, with gills. Dolphins are mammals, like us. They have warm blood, and lungs for breathing air. Kept under water, they would drown. A dolphin comes to the surface and breathes through its blowhole. This is its nose opening, on the top of its head.

12

Turtles live in water, but they have lungs and breathe air just as birds and dolphins do. So they need to come to the surface to take in fresh air. The **green turtle** is one of seven types of sea turtle. The others include the leatherback, hawksbill, and loggerhead turtles. A green turtle can stay under the water for as long as an hour before it needs another breath of air.

Many other water creatures besides fish have gills for taking in oxygen from the water. An **octopus** has gills in the lower part of its "head", which is really its whole body. The gills and other body parts are covered by a large, cloak-shaped flap of skin called the mantle.

Like all fish, the **great white shark** has gills on the sides of its head. The shark swims along with its mouth wide open. Water flows into its mouth, over the gills, and out through the row of gill slits on its "neck". Except, that is, when the shark bites, and its mouth is full of food. It must swallow the food quickly, or it will suffocate.

13

Leave us clues?

They did. But not on purpose, of course. As dinosaurs lived and died, they left behind parts of their bodies and signs of their lives. Soft body parts, such as the flesh, soon rotted away. Harder parts, such as bones, teeth, claws, horns, skin, and eggs, lasted longer. Some of these have been preserved in the rocks for millions of years and have turned to stone. We call them fossils. Experts find and dig up these fossils. They use them as clues to work out how dinosaurs looked, lived, were born, got old, and died.

Fossil bones can tell us a lot about an animal. Skull bones from inside the head provide good clues. The holes in the skull show the size and shape of the dinosaur's brain, eyes, ears, and mouth. This long, narrow fossil skull was dug out of the desert. It has a very large brain case so the dinosaur it belonged to, **Dromiceiomimus** (dro-miss-ee-oh-my-mus), must have been brainy!

Animal teeth are very hard and tough. In fact, they are usually the hardest parts of the body so they often get preserved as fossils. This is lucky, because the shape of the teeth gives clues to what the animal ate. **Heterodontosaurus** (het-er-oh-dont-oh-saw-rus) had teeth of different shapes, which was unusual for a dinosaur. This means it probably ate lots of different foods.

14

Claws and nails, like teeth, are hard parts of the body that do not rot away easily. They last well and, over a long time, can turn into fossils. Claws are clues to the way an animal lived. Long, sharp claws meant that the dinosaur could rip and tear. **Herrerasaurus** (<u>herra</u>-ra-<u>saw</u>-rus) was one of the first dinosaurs. It had long finger claws, so perhaps it grabbed small animals to eat.

Dinosaurs left behind other things that have become fossils, too. Sometimes their droppings went dry and hard, became covered by dust or mud, and were preserved. Huge dinosaurs, such as **Riojasaurus**, (ree-<u>ok</u>-a-<u>saw</u>-rus) left huge piles of dino-dung. The bits and pieces in the droppings, such as pieces of twigs and seeds, are clues to what the dinosaur ate. Luckily, after millions of years, the dung has turned to stone so it doesn't smell!

Even footprints can become clues! When dinosaurs walked on sand or mud, the prints they left sometimes became hard and fossilized. This is how we know that dinosaurs such as **Camarasaurus** (<u>kam</u>-ar-a-<u>saw</u>-rus) lived in groups. The dinosaurs left many tracks as the herd walked along together.

15

Live in towns and cities?

Adults and children all over the world live in towns and cities. In some cities there are millions of people. Many other creatures live together in big groups, too. Usually animals that live together are good neighbors and all work for the benefit of the whole town. They collect and store food, build and look after homes, find new partners, raise their families, and chase away enemies. But, just as in the towns and cities where people live, there are sometimes arguments and even fights.

Puffins are tubby sea birds with big heads and colorful beaks. They nest together in "towns", called colonies, along the seashore. Here, most puffin parents dig a burrow for their eggs. Others take over a spare rabbit hole or a tunnel left by another sea bird. Puffin colonies are always noisy places, full of activity.

Welcome to wasp city. It is a nest the size of a basketball with about 1,000 **wasps** inside. Wasps build the nest from paper that they make from wood. First they scrape up the wood with their jaws. Then they chew it into a sticky liquid. Finally the wasps spread out this liquid, which hardens to make the papery nest walls. Wasps build their nest cities inside a roof or hollow tree.

16

On the grasslands of North America, small heads sometimes pop out of holes in mounds of earth. These heads belong to **prairie dogs**. They make dog-like barks, but they are really a type of squirrel. Each prairie dog family has its own entrance hole leading to its own set of long, deep burrows. More than 10,000 prairie dogs may live in one township. Prairie dog sentries guard the burrows. If they see an enemy, they lift up their heads and bark a warning to all the other inhabitants of the town.

Termites are tiny, soft insects. They live together in groups of over a million. Their cities, called termite mounds, have more inhabitants than any others in the animal world. Inside these giant heaps of hard mud and earth, there are many tunnels and chambers. Here the termites are safe from enemies. The mounds can be twice as high as a person. They're termite skyscrapers!

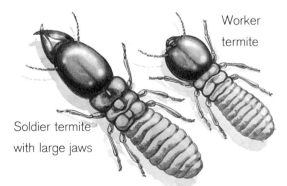

Worker termite

Soldier termite with large jaws

17

Stay so small?

There are many reasons. The bodies of many bugs have a hard outer casing. It is like a skeleton on the outside. This protects and supports the animal. If a bug grows too big, the casing would become too heavy to move or it may even crack! Another reason is that bugs breathe through air tubes. These go from the surface of the body to the inside. If the tubes were too long, the bug would not get air into its body quickly enough and it would suffocate. Also, it takes large animals much longer to become adults and they need to find much more food. So why not become an adult, breed and produce young while still small? For these reasons, and others, bugs stay small.

The **fairy fly wasp**, one of the tiniest insects, looks like a fly. This wasp is so small that it would fit inside this 'o'. It can hide from its enemies in the tiniest crevice. But smallness has its problems, too. You can't fight back against predators, as they are all bigger than you!

What's that small cloud flickering among the trees on a warm summer's evening? It is a swarm of **midges**. Thousands of them flit and fly together, dancing and courting and mating in midair. Midges are types of tiny flies. Some feed on plant juices. Others bite animals, including people, and suck their blood and body fluids. The bite leaves a small, red, itchy spot. Midges stay small because it means they can move around easily to find food.

18

The **Goliath beetle** is about as big as a bug can grow – it can reach a length of 4 inches (11 centimeters). If it were any larger, the Goliath beetle wouldn't be able to move at all. Its outer casing is very thick, like armor-plating. This means the beetle is heavier than any other insect, more than 3 ounces (100 grams). So the Goliath beetle cannot run fast. But its thick armor is good protection against its enemies in the tropical forests of Africa.

Although mites are very small, they have a big effect on the lives of plants and animals. Mites are found almost everywhere. They are arachnids. This means they have eight legs and are cousins of spiders and scorpions. There are thousands of kinds of mites. Some pierce plants to suck sap. Some bite animals to drink blood. These tiny **red mites** are hitchhiking a ride on a spider's leg!

The **elephant hawk moth** is the jumbo jet of the insect world. Its wings are almost 3 inches (about 7 centimeters) across. Like all moths and butterflies, it hatches from its egg as a caterpillar. As caterpillars grow, they shed their skins. The skin underneath needs time to harden. If they were any bigger, the casing might bend or crack before it could harden.

19

Need to drink water?

All animals need water to stay alive. No creature can survive without it. But not all animals need to drink water. Some can get the water they need from their food. This might be the watery saps and juices in plant food, or the blood and body fluids in animal food. Many desert animals get water in this way. They also lose very little water from their bodies in their sweat, urine, and droppings. However, when they find a pool, these animals drink as much as they can.

The **fennec fox** is the world's smallest fox. It is about the size of a pet cat and it lives in the Sahara and Arabian deserts. Like many desert animals, it saves as much of its body water as possible. It produces little urine, and its feces, or droppings, are dry and hard. The huge ears listen for the tiny scrabblings of prey, such as mice and beetles. The fox's ears also help it to lose extra body heat.

The **camel** is well adapted for life in the desert. Its thick fur protects it from the heat and sunburn. Its wide feet stop it from sinking into the sand, and its long eyelashes keep windblown sand out of its eyes. When it finds water, at a well or in the pool of an oasis, a camel can drink 160 quarts (150 liters) in five minutes. That's almost two bathtubs-full.

20

Ostriches are the biggest birds in the world. They live in the savannah grasslands and semi-desert areas of Africa. They feed on leaves, shoots, flowers, and seeds, and get the fluid they need from their food. Ostriches can survive most conditions, as long as there are enough plants to eat.

The **thorny devil** lives in the desert regions of Australia. This lizard "drinks" through its skin. During the cool night, dew forms on the ground and on the thorny devil's skin. Small grooves in its skin soak up water from the ground, and the network of fine grooves funnels this moisture to the lizard's mouth.

The Namib desert, in southwest Africa, is near the coast, where fog and mist blow in from the sea. The **Namib desert beetle** drinks by standing, head down, on a sand dune. Misty moisture droplets from the sea roll down its body into its mouth.

The **Arabian oryx** lives in the deserts of the Middle East. In the heat of the day this small antelope finds shade under acacia trees. It scrapes the dry soil with its hooves to uncover food and moisture. In the night, when it's cooler, the oryx can walk up to 18 miles (30 kilometers) to find new feeding places.

Tower over trees?

Yes, some of them did. The largest dinosaurs were the sauropods. They had a huge barrel-shaped body, stumpy legs, a long whip-like tail, and a long neck with a tiny head. If they reared up and stretched their head and neck, they could reach more than 65 feet (20 meters) into the air. They would have towered over many trees.

Not all dinosaurs were giants. Tiny **Saltopus** (salt-oh-pus) was about the size of a chicken. Being small can be a good thing. Saltopus could have easily hidden from its enemies, among rocks, in a cave or in the under-growth. Also, it would not have needed to eat lots of food, as huge dinosaurs did.

Seismosaurus (size-mo-saw-rus) may have been the longest dinosaur. An adult was over 130 feet (40 meters) from nose to tail-tip, about as long as 10 family cars in a line. Seismosaurus probably swung its head, at the end of its long neck, to reach leaves high in the trees. Or perhaps to feed on plants on the ground.

22

Torosaurus

(<u>tor</u>-oh-<u>saw</u>-rus) could not tower over trees, but it had the biggest head of any dinosaur. In fact, the biggest head of any land animal that ever lived. The huge skull bones, and the large "flap" or frill over its neck, were over 7 feet (2.4 meters) long. That's the size of a large dining table!

Microceratops (my-cro-<u>serra</u>-tops) was a tiny dinosaur, about as long as a pet cat. It probably ran quickly on its two back legs. It belonged to the ceratopsian or "horn face" dinosaur group, so it was a close relative of huge Torosaurus (left).

The famous **Tyrannosaurus rex** (ty-<u>ran</u>-oh-<u>saw</u>-rus reks) was one of the biggest of all meat-eating dinosaurs. It was so tall, about 20 feet (6 meters) high when standing upright, that it could tower over a small tree. But it probably ran in a head-down position. Its huge head and sharp teeth then balanced the heavy tail over its back legs.

23

Go to school?

Many animals are born tiny and helpless. They can do almost nothing except eat, sleep, and grow... just like you when you were a baby. As animals get older, they must learn all kinds of important skills, such as how to hunt and how to escape from danger. Some animals learn from their parents. Others, such as bugs, know what to do from the day they are born. This knowledge is called instinct, but animals still need to practice their skills to make sure they get it right.

These caterpillars are looking for a safe place to spend the night. They are called **processionary moth caterpillars** because they walk in a long line, called a procession. The leader makes sure no one gets lost by leaving a trail of smelly liquid along the branches. So the most important lesson for these caterpillars to learn is to follow their noses!

Chimpanzees learn quickly and they can also solve tricky problems. Young chimps learn to poke sticks into the nests of small insects called termites. They pull out the sticks and lick off the juicy termites. Chimpanzees learn how to do this from their parents and other group members. They may also discover how to use leaves and stones as tools.

24

Honey bees have many different jobs. First, they learn to clean out their hive. Then they practice flapping their wings and blowing air around the hive to keep it cool. Finally, they discover how to collect sweet, sticky nectar from flowers.

Collector bee

Cooler bee

Cleaner bee

Snow geese go to flying school. Every year, these beautiful birds fly to the far north, where they build nests and have their young. Then, before the cold winter, they fly back to the south. For the first few years, young birds follow the older ones who have made the journey before. The youngsters learn to recognize the rivers, mountains, coastlines, islands, and other places on their trip. Soon they are able to find the way on their own.

Baby **otters** have fun splashing around in rivers, playing with sticks and stones. But they are actually learning to be champion swimmers. They need to dart through the water to catch fresh fish. If they don't work hard, they will end up with nothing for dinner.

25

DID DINOSAURS...
Lay eggs?

Yes, they did. Dinosaurs belonged to a group of scaly skinned animals called reptiles. Crocodiles, lizards, turtles, and snakes are all reptiles. Most female reptiles lay eggs that hatch into babies. As dinosaurs were reptiles, they laid eggs too. Experts have dug up fossil eggs buried millions of years ago. They have even found the fossil remains of a dinosaur called Oviraptor sitting on its nest and eggs.

Fossil hunters first found fossil dinosaur eggs in 1922, in the Gobi Desert in Mongolia. The eggs were laid millions of years ago by **Protoceratops** (pro-toh-serra-tops), a dinosaur about the size of a pig. The female Protoceratops scraped a hole in the sand. Then she laid about 30 potato-sized eggs, arranging them neatly in a spiral.

Maiasaura (my-a-saw-ra) was as long as a double-decker bus. It had a wide, flat mouth, like the bill of a duck, and no front teeth. Huge groups of these dinosaurs made nests in the ground, covering entire hillsides. The females laid eggs in hollows scooped out of the earth or mud. They may also have brought food to the nest for their babies to eat.

Some dinosaurs may have protected their eggs and their newly hatched young. **Styracosaurus** (sty-<u>rak</u>-oh-<u>saw</u>-rus) was a large dinosaur, bigger than a car, with long, sharp horns on its head. Few other animals would have tried to attack and eat it. But if a hungry, hunting dinosaur came near, the young dinosaurs could have been at risk. To protect them, the adults might have formed a circle, facing outward with their horns toward the attacker. The young dinosaurs would have stayed in the center, safe from danger.

Eggs are a good food. Many animals today, such as snakes and mongooses (and people), eat them. Some dinosaurs probably ate the eggs of other dinosaurs. **Oviraptor** (<u>ohv</u>-ih-<u>rap</u>-tor) was a speedy, dog-sized dinosaur with long, strong fingers. It lived at the same time and in the same place as Protoceratops. It might have stolen eggs from Protoceratops' nests.

27

Have lots of legs?

To run fast? Yes, sometimes. Some bugs, such as the millipede, have hundreds of legs, but move very slowly. For other bugs, having lots of legs gets them out of all sorts of trouble – they can run or jump away from enemies with ease. Various types of bug bodies and legs have evolved over millions of years to suit different environments. Insects have six legs. Spiders, scorpions, and other arachnids have eight. Centipedes and millipedes have dozens. Some bugs, such as worms, don't have any legs at all!

All insects have six legs, but these are not always the same in shape or size. Legs are not always used in the same way, either. Crickets and grasshoppers, such as the **creosote bush grasshopper**, have long, strong back legs. They use them to leap high and far, to escape from danger. The legs have other interesting uses, too. By rubbing them on other body parts, some grasshoppers and crickets make their chirping song.

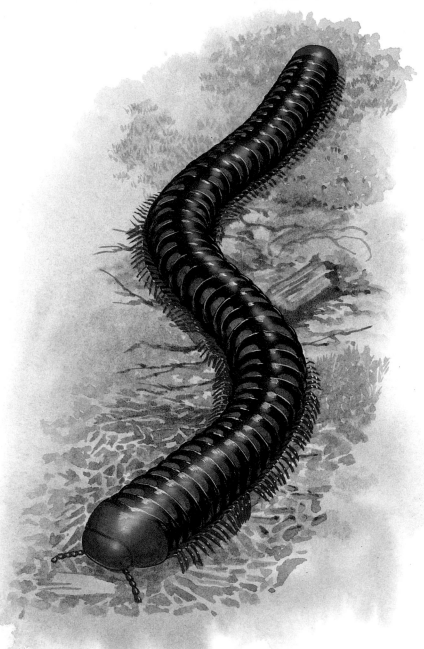

The name millipede means "thousand-legged". But even this **giant millipede** does not have 1,000 legs. Most millipedes have between 100 and 300 legs. Each leg moves back and then forward, slightly after the leg in front. This shows as a wave-like pattern moving along the side of the body. A millipede seems to glide along, as though on lots of tiny wheels.

28

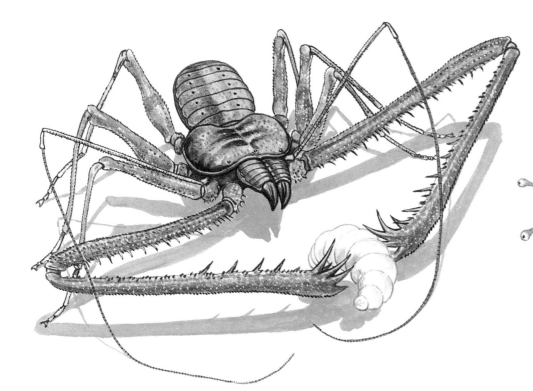

Many **great black slugs** are black. But some are other colors, even orange! Slugs and snails are mollusks. They do not have legs, but they do have a foot. This is the flat, sticky base of the body. The slug slides along with tiny, wave-like ripples of the muscles in its foot. It sticks to smooth ground surfaces by producing a liquid called mucus. This slime is left behind as a shiny trail.

The **tailless whip scorpion** has eight legs, just as other scorpions do. But it only uses six for walking. The front pair of legs are much longer and thinner. They are feelers, used for finding the way by touch. The whip scorpion also has two huge, long and powerful pincers in front of the feeler legs. These pincers are used to grab its prey.

The **cave centipede** runs swiftly on its long, thin legs. It also uses them to feel its surroundings, as it cannot see in the dark caves where it lives. Centipedes are fast, fearsome hunters of tiny animals. They have two legs on each segment, or body section. Millipedes are slower. They eat plants and rotting foods, and they have four legs on each body segment.

29

DO ANIMALS...
Live under the ground?

Yes, many do. Some live almost their entire lives under the ground. They rarely come up to the surface. They eat, rest, feed, and breed in the dark world below your feet. Other animals make tunnels and burrows for their shelters and nests. They usually come out into the open air to find food and a mate. Some creatures make their homes deep in dark holes and caves. These underground homes are usually safe from the animal's enemies. The creatures living there are also protected from the worst of the weather.

The **groundhog**, or woodchuck, spends half the year in a very deep sleep, called hibernation, inside its burrow. The groundhog hibernates during winter, when food is scarce. Legend says it comes out on Groundhog Day, February 2nd, but the groundhog does not have a calendar or diary!

The **European mole** comes to the surface now and then, often after it has rained. It searches for worms and slugs among the damp plants. Most of the time, the mole looks after its tunnels, which may total over 600 feet (200 meters) in length. It keeps the tunnels open, and eats the tiny creatures that live in the earth walls.

30

Many animals make burrows and holes. They usually have body parts that are adapted for digging. Can you guess how the **spadefoot toad** got its name? Each back foot has a flattened side, like a tiny shovel. The toad can dig itself straight down into loose soil and disappear in less than 20 seconds!

The **tuatara** is a type of reptile from New Zealand. It lives on a few rocky islands off the coast. This strange creature looks like a lizard, but it isn't. It belongs to a group of reptiles that were common millions of years ago, even before dinosaurs walked the Earth. Each tuatara lives in a burrow. It often shares its home with a petrel or other sea bird. The tuatara goes out at night to eat spiders and beetles, and the bird goes in for a night's rest!

Surely birds like to fly in the sky and perch in trees, rather than be dark and cramped? Not all birds. **Burrowing owls** live in dry grasslands. There are no trees for perching. So these small owls shelter and raise their chicks in a burrow. But they don't dig the burrow. They use an empty one, or they borrow or steal a ready-made burrow from another animal.

31

Have no teeth?

Yes, it's true. Bugs do not have teeth. That is, they don't have true teeth, like the teeth belonging to humans, cats, dogs, snakes, and some fish. Of course, bugs have mouths for eating and drinking. And the mouths have various parts for getting the food into the body. These parts are simply called mouthparts. The way a bug's mouthparts look and work depends on how the bug feeds. Some bug mouthparts are shaped like fangs, spears, daggers, or pincers. Others are like needles, suckers, sponges, or even drinking straws.

Proboscis coiled for flying

Proboscis uncoiled for feeding

If you drink a thick milk shake through a hollow straw, you have to suck hard. Butterflies, such as this **red admiral**, and moths do the same. Of course, they don't usually drink milk shakes! They sip and suck a thick, sweet liquid, called nectar, from flowers. A butterfly's mouthparts are shaped like a drinking straw and are called a proboscis. When the butterfly is not feeding, the proboscis is coiled up under its head.

All spiders have two sharp, fearsome fangs to stab and kill their victims. The **trap-door spider** has very large fangs. The fangs are black and shiny and are on the front of the spider's head. Its tiny mouth is just behind the fangs. Each fang is fixed to a short, furry part of the mouth, which has a hole through it leading to the fang. The spider jabs the fangs into its prey, and injects venom through the holes and fangs. Few creatures escape the fangs of death!

Fangs

If you spill a drink or some juicy food, you might mop it up with a sponge. This is how flies, such as the **bluebottle**, feed. Their mouthparts are shaped like a sponge-on-a-stalk. First the fly oozes digestive juices from its mouth onto the food. This makes the food runny and watery, like soup. Then the fly dabs its spongy mouthparts onto the soupy food and mops it up.

Your teeth and jaws would soon wear away if you ate nothing but solid wood. Yet that is what the **death watch beetle** eats. Its mouthparts are like strong pincers that move from side to side on powerful jaws. The beetle chews, bores and tunnels its way through the solid wood and emerges from a small hole. At breeding time the beetle taps its jaws on the wood to attract a mate.

Sap is the "blood" of a plant. It flows through tubes inside the stems, stalks, and leaves. It is sweet and full of nutrients and goodness – excellent food! Many bugs, such as these **aphids**, have a sap-sucking way of life. The mouthparts of an aphid are shaped like a tiny, hollow dagger. The aphid jabs this through the plant's outer layer into a sap-carrying tube and drinks its fill.

33

DO ANIMALS...
Have refrigerators?

People keep their food fresh in gleaming
refrigerators. Animals don't have these,
of course, but many creatures do store food
in special hiding places, to make sure they
have enough to eat all year round. In autumn,
when trees are covered with fruits, nuts,
and berries, animals collect and bury
food for the long winter ahead. If you
had to collect or hunt for food,
instead of buying it from the store,
you might do the same!

A **squirrel** rushes about in the autumn gathering nuts and
burying them here, there, and everywhere. During the winter,
when the trees are bare, the squirrel sniffs and digs, and
finds perhaps half of the nuts it hid. The other nuts are not all
wasted. Some grow into new trees.

A **crocodile** sometimes catches
a zebra or an antelope. This is
far too big for one meal. So the crocodile
eats as much as it can, then pushes the
leftovers under a rock or log in the river. The
meat stays safely in place and softens in the
warm water. A few days later, the croc comes
back for a second helping.

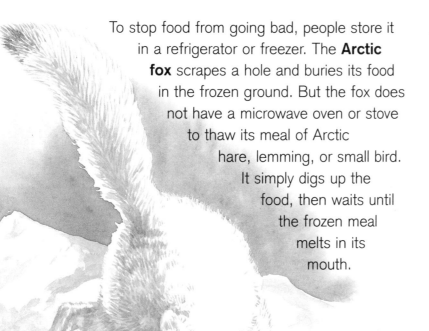

To stop food from going bad, people store it in a refrigerator or freezer. The **Arctic fox** scrapes a hole and buries its food in the frozen ground. But the fox does not have a microwave oven or stove to thaw its meal of Arctic hare, lemming, or small bird. It simply digs up the food, then waits until the frozen meal melts in its mouth.

If some animals didn't eat droppings and dung, the world would be full of it! The favorite food of the **dung beetle** is warm, moist, freshly produced dung. The bcetle rolls dung up in a ball, lays eggs in it, and hides the ball in a burrow. When the eggs hatch, the beetle grubs have their food waiting.

The **shrike** is a fierce hunter of insects, small lizards, frogs, mice, and other little creatures. On a good day, it catches more victims than it can eat at once. So it sticks the extra ones on to thorns or plant spines, then comes back later for a snack. This gruesome larder of hanging meat gives the shrike its other name – the butcher bird.

35

DID DINOSAURS...
Run quickly?

Have you seen a reptile, such as a small lizard, which is warm from sunbathing? It can run so fast that it seems to disappear in a flash. Dinosaurs were reptiles, so they could probably run fast, too. To do this, their bodies would have to be warm from the heat of the sun. When a reptile gets cold it moves more slowly. The fastest dinosaurs had long, slim back legs – the same design as the very speedy bird, the ostrich. A dinosaur with short, thick legs probably lumbered along slowly.

Coelophysis (<u>seel</u>-oh-<u>fy</u>-sis) was one of the thinnest and slimmest of the dinosaurs. It was about 10 feet (3 meters) long and about 3 feet (one meter) high, yet it weighed only 55 pounds (25 kilograms). By flicking its head and neck one way, and its tail the other way, it could probably turn around instantly to chase its prey.

Struthiomimus (<u>stroo</u>-thee-oh-<u>my</u>-mus) was named after the ostrich of today. The name means "ostrich mimic" since it was almost exactly the same size and shape as an ostrich. So Struthiomimus may have been able to run as fast as an ostrich, which is up to 50 miles (80 kilometers) per hour.

Ankylosaurus

(an-<u>ky</u>-lo-<u>saw</u>-rus)
was probably one of
the slowest dinosaurs.
But this didn't matter. Its
body was very well protected by
large lumps and plates of bone in its skin.
Only its underbelly was soft. This armor was
heavy, but Ankylosaurus had no need for speed.

Brachiosaurus

(<u>brak</u>-ee-oh-<u>saw</u>-rus) was
so heavy that it could not
race along as horses do. It
probably plodded like an
elephant. Its legs were wide
and strong, just like an
elephant's legs, but much
larger! Brachiosaurus was
one of the biggest
dinosaurs ever. It was over
80 feet (25 meters) long
and stood up to 60 feet
(18 meters) tall on its long
front legs. It weighed over
65 tons (60 tonnes) – as
much as two huge trucks.

Ceratosaurus

(<u>ser</u>-a-toh-<u>saw</u>-rus) had
the body shape of a
fast-running dinosaur. It
had a slim head, a long
body, short front legs,
very long, strong back
legs, and a long tail for
balance. Ceratosaurus
weighed as much as a
hippopotamus, but it
could probably run much
faster than a hippo.

37

Play in the waves?

Do you enjoy the seaside? You can paddle and splash, and have fun in the sun. But would you like to live there even in winter? We are not really adapted to seashore life. But many animals thrive on the coast. They do not mind the hot sun or the cold wind and rain. They can survive being covered by salt water as the tide comes in. They can also survive being dry as the tide goes out. Such animals live on the seashore all the time. They are adapted to life in this ever-changing habitat. Other animals just come to the shore to rest or feed.

Limpets

Mussels

Whelk

Many creatures that live in rock pools have hard shells to protect their soft bodies. They are called mollusks. The **limpets** cling so strongly to the rock that not even a huge wave can knock them off. The **mussels** are fixed to the rock by stringy threads, and they filter the sea water for food. The **whelk**, a type of sea snail, then eats the mussels!

Common seals feed in the ocean, chasing fish and other sea creatures. When the sun comes out they swim to the beach. They wriggle and heave themselves out of the water to sunbathe on the sand. But they keep a sharp watch for trouble, especially at breeding time. A seal pup can swim well just a few minutes after it is born. Like other baby mammals, it feeds on its mother's milk. It can drink this on land, or in the water.

Many birds live along seashores. They have long legs to wade through the waves and shallows, and long beaks to probe for food in the sand and mud. **Oystercatchers** feed on oysters, and also on mussels, clams, and similar shellfish. They peck hard at the shells to make a hole, then eat the soft flesh inside.

Shore fish, such as the **rock goby**, are very tough. They have to cope with crashing waves, rolling stones, moving sand, and being stranded as the tide goes out. The goby has thick, slippery skin and strong, spiny fins. It can skip and slither across the slimy rocks, out of the water, from one pool to another.

Recycling is a good idea, and **shore crabs** are nature's recyclers on the seashore. They are scavengers. They eat all kinds of plants and animals, whether sick, dying, or dead. Then the crabs themselves become food for birds, fish, and other sea creatures.

39

DID DINOSAURS...
Have wings?

No. There were no flying dinosaurs.
But there were other flying creatures
that lived at the same time. These
included dragonflies, and other
insects, and the pterosaurs
(<u>ter</u>-oh-<u>sors</u>) or "winged reptiles".
Pterosaurs looked very much like
dinosaurs with wings, but they
weren't dinosaurs. They belonged
to a different group of reptiles.
Also, the first birds appeared during
the Age of Dinosaurs. So the skies
were probably quite crowded.

Dimorphodon
(dy-<u>morf</u>-oh-don)
was a pterosaur. It
had a large beak-like
mouth, and it probably flew
over the waves and grabbed fish
from just below the water's surface. Its
wings measured over 4 feet (1.4 meters)
from one tip to the other. Its long tail
helped to balance and steer it in flight.

Archaeopteryx (<u>ar</u>-kee-<u>op</u>-ter-ix) was the first bird, as
far as we know from fossils. Its fossil bones, beak, and
feathers have been found preserved in great detail. Its
skeleton is very similar to that of a small dinosaur. But
feathers are the key. Any animal with feathers is a bird.

Compsognathus (komp-sog-<u>nay</u>-thus) was one of the
smallest dinosaurs. But its tail was actually as long as the
rest of its body. It was slim and light, and it could run very
fast. It is possible that some kinds of dinosaurs like
Compsognathus slowly changed over time into the first birds.

Quetzalcoatlus (<u>kwet</u>-zal-<u>koht</u>-lus) was the biggest pterosaur and probably glided on the mountain winds. With wings measuring 40 feet (12 meters) across, it was the size of a small aircraft! Yet its body was very light, because many of its bones were tube-like and filled with air. Most pterosaurs had light bones like these.

Pterodaustro (<u>ter</u>-oh-<u>dow</u>-stro) had a long beak-like mouth. The top jaw had a few teeth in it, but the lower jaw had lots of springy bristles instead. This pterosaur may have stood in shallow water and swished its mouth back and forth in the water. It could then swallow any small creatures trapped in the bristles. The great whales of today, like blue whales, feed this way.

Avimimus (<u>av</u>-i-<u>my</u>-mus) is a puzzling dinosaur. Some experts say that tiny marks on its fossil bones show where its feathers were attached. If so, Avimimus might have been a bird, not a dinosaur. The general shape of its skeleton was also very similar to the skeleton of a bird.

41

Wear spots and stripes?

Yes, many animals have spotted or striped coats. These colored patterns help the animals to blend in with their background. We say that they are camouflaged. Such camouflage helps an animal to hide and survive. A predator that cannot easily be seen, can creep up unnoticed on its prey. The camouflaged prey can hide from the hunter! Which one wins depends on which animal is quietest or most stealthy. Or, if it comes to a chase, which one can run the fastest.

The **pampas cat** lives in the grasslands, scrubs, and forests of South America. This medium-sized cat creeps through the dark night, eating any small animals it can catch. It feeds on insects, mice, rats, and other small mammals, birds, lizards, and their eggs. The cat's dark spots help to disguise its body shape in the shadows of the moonlit undergrowth. A pet tabby cat is blotched and striped for the same reason.

Few animals are as striped as a **zebra**! This close relation of the horse has black stripes on a white background – or is it the other way round? The zebra blends in with the tall grasses, and their shadows, on the savannahs of Africa. Zebras live in groups or herds. When they spot danger, they panic and run. A predator, such as a lion, has great trouble picking out one victim from the flashing, dazzling mass of moving stripes!

42

Some animals have glaring spots or stripes. These are not for camouflage, but for showing off and being seen clearly. The **ladybug** is one. Its bright patterns are called warning colors. They warn other animals that a ladybug tastes horrible. Birds and other animals soon learn this, and they leave ladybugs alone.

Hyenas have stripes and spots, but not on the same animal. The **striped hyena** (shown here) lives in northern Africa, the Middle East, and India. The spotted hyena has spots instead of stripes. It lives in the grasslands of east and southern Africa. Both types of hyena are fierce hunters and scavengers. Their patterns are mainly for camouflage. They help the hyenas blend in among the dry grasses.

Some creatures are so huge and strong that they do not need disguise or camouflage. The **rhinoceros** is the world's second biggest land animal, and it has a very plain color. Its main defenses are size, weight, a very thick skin, and a sharp nose horn. Hardly any predators dare to attack it. If they do, they get speared by its horn and trampled under its massive body.

43

DO ANIMALS...

Eat take-out meals?

If people do not want to cook a meal, they can order food from a take-out restaurant. When it is ready, they carry the food home in special containers. Some animals also collect their food packed in containers, ready to eat, and perhaps still warm. But the containers are hairy or scaly and there are often bits of bone in the food. Animals cannot just order food – they have to catch their take-out meals before they can carry them home.

A mouse, vole, or lemming is a small snack for a grown-up **owl**, but the same victim makes a meal for an owl chick. The parent owls are busy all night. They swoop through the dark to grab furry bundles of food, which they carry back to a nestful of hungry owlets.

In North America, **raccoons** sometimes visit houses and search through garbage cans. These animals sniff around everywhere, looking for leftover food. Raccoons will eat almost anything, from bites of burger to chicken bones and French fries. Often they grab scraps from take-out meal cartons and hurry away with them – secondhand take-outs!

44

Rabbits don't take their food home, but they certainly eat it from special containers! Rabbits spend many hours nibbling grass and leaves, and take in goodness from them. They get rid of the leftovers as small, round droppings on the ground. Later, they eat these droppings to take in any minerals they missed the first time round. When the rabbits produce droppings for the second time, these are much drier and harder.

The **bolas spider** does not spin a web. Instead it hangs around on a twig or rock, waiting for unwary insects to wander past. Then it leaps out, lassoes an insect with a silk rope, and ties its prey into a neat bundle. The spider's name comes from the bolas, a rope with weights at the end that South American cowboys use to trip up cattle.

The favorite take-out of the **fisherman bat** is fish. Almost every evening the bat swoops over rivers and lakes, watching for ripples made by fish just below the surface. Then it grabs a victim with its long-clawed feet and flies away to a tree. There it tears the meat from its instant, slippery, scaly snack.

Bite and sting?

Is it just to annoy you or even hurt you? No, not really. Bugs go about their business looking for food and nesting places, and trying to breed. If an animal tries to stop them or harm them, then they fight back, using whatever means they can. Some bugs have powerful venoms to make up for their tiny size. They sting or bite when they think that their lives are in danger, perhaps from a gigantic creature, such as you, who is about to kill them. Of course, some bugs bite because you are their food – or they think you are!

The **green scorpion** is a fast runner, and the sharp sting at the end of its tail can inject venom. This bug uses venom mainly for self-defense or to stop its prey from struggling. Scorpions sometimes come into houses to feed on the insects attracted by food or the house lights. So if you are in a hot climate it's always wise to check before you sit down – in case there is a green scorpion lurking!

When a bee, such as this **bumblebee**, stings you, that's the last thing it will ever do. The sting's backward-pointing barb sticks in the victim. The whole sting and venom bag are ripped from the rear of the bee's body, and the bee soon dies. But the sacrifice is worthwhile to protect the rest of the bee's nest against intruders. This bumblebee is ready to defend its nest, but the mouse quickly runs away.

46

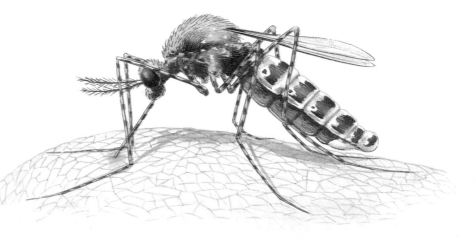

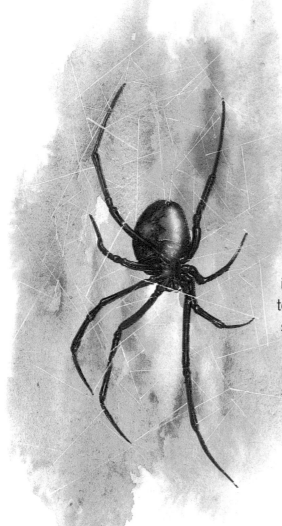

If you ever see this creature, get out of the way at once! It's a **black widow spider**. It may be small, but its venomous bite can be deadly to animals and humans alike. However, its venom is used mainly to kill its insect food. The spider jabs its fangs into a victim and injects the venom. Its prey is soon still and quiet. While it's still alive its insides get dissolved by the juices from the bite!

By the time you feel a **mosquito** on your skin, it is already drinking your blood, which is its food. This insect's mouth is like a sharp-tipped drinking straw. It slides its mouthparts through the top layer of your skin. The mosquito's saliva stops your blood from clotting as it bites and sucks. This saliva also causes the itchy red spot you get afterwards.

Huge, antler-shaped jaws give the **stag beetle** its name. It looks as if these beetles could give you a nasty bite. But the jaws are so heavy, and the muscles that move them are so weak, that the beetle can hardly bite at all. The jaws are for show and for battling with other males. The male stag beetles grapple and push each other to impress females.

47

Go on vacation?

Most people like to travel to sunny places for their vacations. Animals do too. Many creatures leave cold countries to go somewhere warm for several months each year. Their long journeys are called migrations. Once they arrive, they can rest and feed. Some animals never stay in one place for long. They are always on the move and every day is a new holiday adventure.

Swallows make sure they are always somewhere warm. In the summer, they live in Europe. Here they build nests, lay eggs and feed their babies on flies, gnats, and other small insects. When it starts to get cold, the swallows take off on their travels to Africa, where they can enjoy warm weather for the rest of the year.

These animals are called **reindeer**. During spring and summer they live in the cold, open lands of northern Europe. When autumn comes, it is too cold even for them, so they go on a winter vacation. They head south in large herds. As the snow melts in spring they walk north again, eating the new, juicy plants as they go.

48

Beautiful **monarch butterflies** are sun-seekers. As summer ends in Canada and the USA they fly south. Some go as far as Mexico. Here thousands of them rest through the warm winter, clustering on cliffs, trees, and cave walls. Next summer they will fly north again.

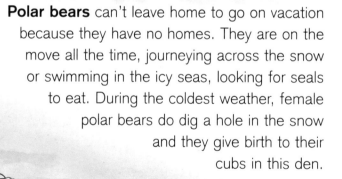

Polar bears can't leave home to go on vacation because they have no homes. They are on the move all the time, journeying across the snow or swimming in the icy seas, looking for seals to eat. During the coldest weather, female polar bears do dig a hole in the snow and they give birth to their cubs in this den.

Some animals' vacations are mystery tours – at least they are a mystery to us! Every autumn in the Caribbean, **spiny lobsters** march in long processions across the sea bed. Slowly, they make their way towards deeper water. Nobody really knows why. Perhaps they are going away to escape stormy seas and strong currents. In a few months they will be back in the shallower seas.

Have scaly skins?

Yes. Fossils of scaly skin have been found with dinosaur bones, teeth, and other remains. The scales were hard enough to be preserved and turned to stone. Also, dinosaurs were reptiles. The reptiles alive today, such as lizards, snakes, and crocodiles, all have scaly skin. Scales are made of a tough, strong material called keratin. A dinosaur's scales protected its body. They also gave the dinosaur's skin its colors and patterns.

Elephant-sized **Stegosaurus** (<u>steg</u>-oh-<u>saw</u>-rus) had scaly skin. It also had huge, flat plates of bone sticking up along its back. It may have had bony shields on its hips, too. These plates of bone helped to protect the dinosaur from attack by meat-eaters. They may also have helped Stegosaurus to control its body temperature, so it did not get too warm or too cold.

Saltasaurus (<u>salt</u>-a-<u>saw</u>-rus) was a huge dinosaur. It had the usual small scales in its skin, but it also had two extra kinds of protection. Small, pea-sized lumps of bone were packed into the skin along the back and sides of Saltasaurus. Larger, higher lumps of bone, as big as your hand, were found on the dinosaur's back.

Carnotaurus (carn-oh-<u>taw</u>-rus) was a meat-eating dinosaur. Pieces of its fossilized skin, showing thousands of scales, have been found. The scales were the size and shape of coins. Carnotaurus also had a strange, pointed, bony horn above each eye.

Stygimoloch (<u>stij</u>-ee-<u>mol</u>-ok) was a "bone-head" dinosaur. It had a thick plate of bone on top of its head, with rows of horns around it. This could have been for protection. Or perhaps it butted its rivals or enemies, as goats do today.

Spinosaurus (<u>spy</u>-no-<u>saw</u>-rus) had an unusual "sail" on its back. It was a flap of scaly skin held up by rods of bone that stuck up from its main backbone. The sail of Spinosaurus may have helped it to control its body temperature by picking up warm sun rays to heat its blood.

51

WHY DO BUGS...
Live underwater?

Lots of animals, from worms and snails to tadpoles and fish, live underwater. They have all life's needs – food, shelter, and breeding partners. For most bugs, living underwater can be difficult, as they need to breathe air. Unlike many other underwater creatures, bugs do not have gills for breathing underwater. A bug's answer is to visit the surface regularly for a supply of air. It stores this air as tiny bubbles around its body. Thousands of kinds of bugs live in ponds, streams, lakes, and rivers – and even the sea.

The **great diving beetle** is the prime predator of the pond. This tiny terror attacks tadpoles, small fish, and similar prey. It breathes air trapped under the hard, shiny wing cases on its back. It swims strongly by rowing with its oar-like legs. Like any other beetle, it can run on land with its legs and fly through the air with its wings.

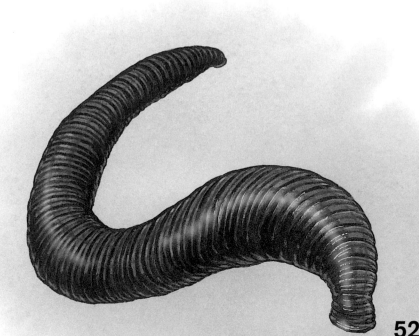

Leeches are flattened relations of earthworms. Many live in water or damp places on land. They stick onto a larger creature, such as a fish or a horse, and suck out its blood and body fluids. The **medicinal leech** was used by doctors in medieval times to suck the blood from sick people. This was supposed to cure them, but often it made them even more ill.

52

Some bugs live on the water instead of under it. The **pond skater** slides across the water's shiny surface, like a person skating on ice. Its tiny weight is held up by surface tension, which forms a "thin skin" on top of the water. The pond skater slides over to tiny creatures trapped in the surface tension. Then the bug spears its prey with its sharp, needle-like mouthparts and sucks out the juices from the victim's body.

You can use a long tube called a snorkel to let you breathe air, while your face is underwater. The **water scorpion** has a kind of snorkel, too. But this breathing tube is on its tail, so its whole body can stay underwater! There is plenty of food in the water for the water scorpion. It hangs around in the weeds of a pond or lake. When a tadpole or similar prey passes by, the bug grabs it in its pincer-like front legs.

Some water insects like the still conditions found in a pond or lake. In a fast stream, the current washes them away and crushes them. But not this **stonefly nymph**, the larva of the stonefly. It clings to the smooth pebbles on the stream bed with its strong, splayed-out legs and hook-like feet.

Like the water scorpion (above) this larva has a breathing tube on its tail. This larva is a maggot – when fully grown it will be a dronefly. Its "snorkel" is so long that it looks like the tail of a rat. That is why it is called a **rat-tailed maggot**. Rat-tailed maggots love dirty, polluted water, just like rats!

53

Hang around in trees?

Forests cover large parts of the world. Huge numbers of animals live in these trees, especially in tropical rain forests. They range from tiny beetles, butterflies, and tree frogs, to large snakes, birds, and monkeys. Some of these creatures rarely come down to the ground. The trees provide all their needs – food of all kinds and drink in the form of rainwater pools trapped in branch forks. Leaves or tree holes provide shelter and there are many places to rest, nest, and raise a family.

The **orangutan** seems to have four arms. It can grip and climb as well with its feet and legs as with its arms. This great ape lives in tropical rain forests on the islands of Borneo and Sumatra in Southeast Asia. The orangutan, often called the "old man of the forest", moves slowly and carefully among the branches. It searches for wild fruits, such as figs, lychees, and mangoes.

If you live among leaves, green is a good color for camouflage. The **green tree python** lies coiled firmly around a branch. It can stay very still for a long, long time. Other creatures forget it's there. If a bird, tree frog, or other animal comes too near, the python quickly grabs its next meal.

Crawl around as slowly as you can, and you still would not be as slow as a **sloth**. This creature is not lazy, just living life at its own speed. Its body is designed for hanging around in the trees of Central and South America. Its claws, like curved hooks, grip the branch tightly. Its fur slants the other way from most mammals, so that rain drips off easily. Sloths eat mainly leaves – slowly, of course.

It can be difficult to find a mate among the crowded leaves and twigs of the rain forest. So the male **blue bird of paradise** finds a small clearing among the branches. Here, he puts on an amazing dancing display. He hangs upside down, shakes his brilliantly colored feathers and sings loudly. Females soon gather, and the male chooses a mate.

If you constantly climb through trees, four limbs may not always be quite enough. So the **tamandua** (tree anteater) has five. The fifth is its tail. The tail is thick, long, muscular, and strong. It is also prehensile, which means it can wrap around and grip objects like a tree branch. Like its ground-living cousins, this anteater feeds on termites and ants. It searches them out both in trees and on the ground.

55

WHY DO BUGS...
Need wings?

For flying! All bugs with wings are insects – moths, flies, beetles and so on. Most insects have two or four wings. They flap them to fly. But why fly? This way of getting about has some good points for small creatures such as insects. They can escape quickly from predators that live on the ground. And flying is far faster than walking or running. This is important when you only have a short time to find food, a place to nest and a mate.

Wing case

Flight wing

The **green lacewing** flies in search of prey. It feeds mainly on aphids, which damage garden plants and farm crops. The "laces" in its wings are veins, strong tubes that carry insect blood. Some of the veins are hollow and pick up the vibrations made by shrill bat squeaks. This helps the lacewing to avoid getting caught.

The **cockchafer** is a big, strong beetle. Like other beetles, it has two pairs of wings. Well, the first pair are not really wings. They are tough, hard, curved wing cases that form the beetle's "back". They protect the second pair of wings, which are folded up underneath them. These flight wings are thin and delicate, like normal insect wings. To fly, the beetle holds up the first pair, and unfolds and flaps the second pair.

The biggest wings in the insect world belong to the rare **Queen Alexandra birdwing butterfly**. This bug has a wing-span of almost 10 inches (about 25 centimeters) and lives in tropical forests in Southeast Asia. Butterflies and moths have four wings. On each side, the two wings are linked by tiny hooks, so they beat together. The wings are almost transparent, but they are covered with thousands of tiny scales, which give them their beautiful colors and patterns.

Flies, such as this **cranefly**, make up a huge group of insects. A fly has only two wings, not four like most insects. This group includes houseflies, horseflies, botflies, blowflies, dungflies, fruitflies, mosquitoes, gnats, midges, and thousands of others. The cranefly is a large fly with long, spindly legs. The legs hang below its body as it flies along, slowly and clumsily.

A few insects, such as this **silverfish**, have no wings. Springtails, bristletails, and firebrats are other wingless insects. These creatures are mostly very small and often move about at night. The silverfish lives in our houses. It feeds on scraps of food and anything else it can eat – even the glue or paste that holds wallpaper on the wall!

57

Wear winter clothes?

In the winter, wild animals, unlike people, do not have the luxury of clothes. They survive the winter cold in any way they can. Many mammals change their natural fur coats in the autumn. The thinner hairs of the summer coat fall out, or molt. Longer, thicker hairs grow in their place. The thick winter coat keeps the animal warm and dry, even in icy winds and heavy snow. Birds molt, too. They lose their summer feathers and grow thicker plumage for the winter.

The thickness of feathers or fur is important. So is color. **Ptarmigans** live in the far north, where the winter landscape is white with frost, snow, and ice. So, in winter, the ptarmigan turns white. Its winter feathers help it to blend in with the background. This camouflage means the ptarmigan cannot be seen so easily. In summer, its brown plumage helps it to blend in among the grasses and twigs.

Siberia, in northern Asia, is one of the world's coldest places, even in summer. The **Siberian tiger** has the longest and thickest fur of any tiger. It is also the world's biggest tiger, more than 11½ feet (3.5 meters) from nose to tail-tip. In winter, its coat is very pale with thin stripes. This helps it to hide in the snow as it creeps up on its prey. Siberian tigers now live only in a small area of northeast Asia, and they are very rare.

Hares are famous for their long ears. But the **snowshoe hare** of North America has quite short ears. Why? Because large body parts that stick out, such as ears and tails, lose a lot of heat. In cold places, animals need to keep in as much body heat as they can. This shows that body shape, as well as a thick, furry coat, is important.

The **musk ox** has very thick, very long fur to keep it warm. Each hair is longer than your arm. Musk oxen live in the far north of North America – from Alaska across to Greenland. The countryside is covered with ice and snow for most of the year. The oxen scrape away the snow with their hooves, to uncover plants to eat.

The **walrus** lives in the Arctic area around the North Pole. It swims in the icy seas and basks on frozen snow in the weak winter sun. But it has hardly any fur at all. So how does it stay warm? Under its skin, the walrus has a very thick layer of body fat, called blubber. This is very good at keeping in body heat. Whales also have thick blubber, for the same reason.

59

Eat grass?

Animals that eat plants are called herbivores. They usually have broad, flat teeth to chew their food well. The shape of some dinosaurs' fossil teeth and jaws suggest that they were herbivores. A few fossil dinosaurs even have the fossilized remains of their last meals in their bodies. But dinosaurs did not eat grass. How do we know? Because no fossil grasses have been found from the Age of Dinosaurs. Grass did not grow until long after dinosaurs died out.

Gallimimus (<u>gal</u>-ih-<u>my</u>-mus) was a tall, thin dinosaur, shaped like a huge ostrich. Its beak-like mouth had no teeth so it could not chew, it could only bite and peck. It probably ate anything it could, including leaves and fruits. It may also have eaten tiny animals such as insects and lizards.

Plateosaurus (<u>plat</u>-ee-oh-<u>saw</u>-rus) was one of the first really large dinosaurs. Its teeth were like small blades, ideal for biting off and slicing up leaves. But it could not chew. This dinosaur might have reared up on its back legs to feed high in trees.

60

The duck-billed dinosaur **Kritosaurus** (<u>cry</u>-toh-<u>saw</u>-rus) had hundreds of teeth near the back of its mouth. They were broad and quite flat, but with sharp edges and ridges. Kritosaurus could probably chew up almost anything, even hard roots and woody stems.

Mamenchisaurus (ma-<u>men</u>-chee-<u>saw</u>-rus) had an extremely long neck. But its head was tiny and it had lots of strong, small teeth. This dinosaur could have swung its head around, and bitten and raked the leaves off trees. But it could not chew them. So Mamenchisaurus also ate stones! It swallowed them, and in its stomach these stones worked like a grinding mill to mash up its leafy food.

61

Bump into each other in the dark?

Not very often. We stumble about and bump into things in the dark. That's because our bodies are adapted to being active by daylight and asleep during darkness. Humans are diurnal. Some animals sleep by day and come out at night. They are nocturnal. They are adapted to finding their way in darkness without a stumble or a bump. Their huge eyes see in very dim light. Their large whiskers feel for objects. Their keen noses sniff food and their sensitive ears hear danger.

Little blue penguins are the smallest penguins, only 12 inches (30 centimeters) tall. They live in tunnels along the seashores of southern Australia. They do not finish fishing and feeding in the sea until after dark. Then they waddle quickly across the beach to the safety of their burrows in the dunes.

The **bushbaby** of African forests was named from its night-time cry. It sounds like the screaming wail of a human baby. This hand-sized relative of monkeys also looks babyish with its huge eyes, which help it to see in the dark, and snub nose. But a crying bushbaby is not in pain. It is warning other bushbabies to keep out of its own small area, or territory, of forest, where it lives and feeds.

62

The **nightjar** is well named. At night it sings its jarring, churring song – it sounds like a small motorcycle engine! At night, too, the nightjar swoops over fields and between trees as it catches its food of flying insects. Its good eyesight and wide beak help this nocturnal hunting. By day, the nightjar sits quite still on the ground or in a tree. It looks like a small pile of dead leaves or a stumpy branch.

Bats, such as the **horseshoe bat**, avoid bumps not by seeing, but by squeaking and listening. The bat makes very high squeaks, clicks, and other sounds. The echoes of these sounds bounce off nearby objects, such as trees and walls or moths and mosquitoes. The bat listens to the pattern of these echoes. It can then find its way or can catch food, even in total darkness.

Most cats, such as this **black panther**, are adapted to hunt at night. They can see well in the dark. On a night with little moonlight, few creatures would see the black panther creeping silently towards them. This big cat is really a very dark-colored type of leopard. Bright daylight reveals its black spots against the slightly paler fur. In parts of Southeast Asia, nearly half of all leopards are black. In Africa, black leopards are much rarer.

63

Give each other presents?

Some animals do give one another presents, but not on birthdays or during special festivals as people do. Creatures usually give presents to their mates when they are courting in spring. An adult sometimes gives its partner a surprise present at other times of the year, just to make sure he or she doesn't forget they are mates. Animal parents give "toys" to their babies to play with. Imagine how disappointed you would be if you opened a package to find just a twig or a stone.

The **right whale** baby is enormous, almost as big as a car. Its mother looks after it well and protects it from hungry enemies, such as sharks and killer whales. The mother may give her baby a present of a tree trunk that has floated out to sea. The baby whale has great fun playing with this huge "toy". It will bash it about in the water with its flippers and tail.

Some birds offer presents to their partners. The gifts are usually pieces of food, and they help the male and female to stay friends. The male **kingfisher** gives his mate a fish. He offers it head-first, so that she can swallow it without choking. These tasty presents help to keep the partners together.

The male **wolf spider** catches a fly or other insect and ties it with his silk thread. Then he gives this neatly wrapped parcel to the female. While she undoes the present and eats it, he quickly mates with her. The male spider is smaller than the female and, at mating time, she may eat him. So it is very important for the male not to forget this present!

Gibbons are long-armed apes that swing through the trees of Southeast Asia. Like many apes and monkeys they groom each other. This means that they comb and scratch through each other's fur and pick out dirt, leaves, and pests. They may offer the pests, such as lice and fleas, to each other to eat as tasty tidbits!

65

DO ANIMALS...

Stay home alone?

Yes, they do. In fact, in the animal world, it is natural and very common for young animals to be left alone. They stay in the nest or burrow while the parents go out to feed. The babies are usually well hidden and know by instinct that they must stay quiet to remain safe from their enemies. Could you stay quiet for half a day until your parents came back? You probably could if your life depended on it!

A young **deer** is called a fawn. Unlike its parents, the fawn has white spots on its fur. As it lies in the grass under a bush, the fawn's pattern merges with the shadows and patches of sunlight. This makes it very hard for enemies to spot the fawn. The mother deer is away feeding, but she will soon return.

The **albatross** is a huge, white sea bird with very long wings. The baby albatross is a large ball of fluffy feathers. Its parents fly over the sea for two or three weeks catching fish. They leave the chick alone on a cold, windy island. But there is a reward. The parents bring back smelly, half-digested fish for their baby to eat.

Baby **penguins** are born in the coldest place on Earth, the ice-covered land of Antarctica. Even a freezer is warmer! The parent penguins waddle off and dive into the ocean to catch fish and other sea animals. The babies are left home alone and stay in a group, huddled together against the cold. They don't need to worry about enemies. It is too cold for any other animals.

Usually, a young **kangaroo** lives in its mother's pouch, which is a pocket of skin on her front. The baby only comes out to play or feed. But the mother may sometimes have to bound away very quickly to avoid enemies. Then she leaves her baby hiding in a bush, so that she can run faster. She returns later to collect her baby.

The **platypus** has webbed feet, a furry body, and a mouth like a duck's bill. It lives in rivers and lakes in eastern Australia. Baby platypuses live in a long tunnel, which the mother digs in a river bank. When she goes out to eat, the mother blocks the burrow entrance with mud. The babies are alone, but safely locked in.

67

Talk to each other?

Not exactly. They didn't speak using words, as we do, but many animals today send messages to others of their kind. Some "sing", making sounds such as hisses, squeaks, and roars. Others "dance", moving about in certain ways. They may also "wave flags", showing off brightly colored parts of their bodies. Other animals understand the messages. They could say "Danger! An enemy is nearby". Or "Stay away from my territory, the land where I live and feed". Or even "Would you like to mate with me?"

The hadrosaur (had-ro-saw) group of dinosaurs had mouths like duck bills. Many hadrosaurs had strange shapes of bone on their heads. **Parasaurolophus** (par-a-saw-ro-lo-fus) was one. It had a long, bony pipe sticking out from its head. Its breathing tubes went through this pipe. Perhaps this dinosaur was able to make trumpeting sounds, as an elephant does through its trunk. It could have called to keep in touch with its herd members as they looked for food.

Chasmosaurus (kaz-mo-saw-rus) belonged to a group called the ceratopsians (serra-top-see-ans), or "horn faces". It had huge frilly-edged flaps of skin on its neck. Imagine if these were brightly colored. The dinosaur could shake its head to send signals to other Chasmosaurus, or even to frighten off enemies.

Corythosaurus (co-rith-oh-<u>saw</u>-rus) was another type of hadrosaur. It had a large, curved plate of bone sticking up from its head. This bony plate was hollow. Perhaps Corythosaurus blew its breathing air through the plate and made a sound like a car horn.

Edmontosaurus (ed-<u>mont</u>-oh-<u>saw</u>-rus) was also a hadrosaur. Marks on its nose bone show that it probably had a flap of skin there. Perhaps it could inflate the skin like a balloon to give a color and sound signal.

Psittacosaurus (si-<u>tak</u>-oh-<u>saw</u>-rus) was a ceratopsian, a relative of Chasmosaurus (opposite). Psittacosaurus means "parrot reptile". It had a very deep, beak-like mouth, just like a parrot or puffin. Perhaps others in its group identified it by the bright stripes on the beak.

As the old saying goes, actions speak louder than words. **Pachycephalosaurus** (<u>pak</u>-ee-<u>sef</u>-al-lo-<u>saw</u>-rus) may have given its message by charging at its enemies and rivals. This dinosaur was unlikely to get hurt. It had a thick layer of bone on top of its head for protection.

69

DO ANIMALS...
Need umbrellas?

Have you been caught out in a rainstorm without a coat or umbrella? You soon get wet and you feel cold and uncomfortable. This is because you are used to being dry, and your body is suited to dry places. Some animals are used to living in water. Their bodies are adapted to the wet. These animals can come out on land, but if they get too dry they soon feel uncomfortable. They are expert swimmers and they catch their food in the water. Some creatures, such as fish, must stay in water all the time. If they come out into the air, they cannot breathe. Within a few minutes they suffocate and die.

Swans are beautiful white birds that float on rivers and lakes. They swim using their webbed feet. Their feathers have a natural oily coating that keeps out water, so the swans stay dry. This bird often combs, or preens, its feathers with its beak. This helps to remove dirt and spread the oil over the swan's feathers.

The **pike** lives in waterweeds. Like all fish, the pike must always stay wet, but its body is protected from the water by a layer of hard scales and waterproof skin. Its gills, on the sides of its head, can only take in oxygen from the water. In air, the gills dry out and the pike dies. As a small fish swims past, the pike flicks its powerful tail, darts out, and opens its huge, sharp-toothed mouth. SNAP, the fish has gone!

Most wild animals can swim if they have to. It's part of being able to survive in nature. The **grass snake** swims well, and goes into water more often than many other snakes. This is because it catches some of its food in the water. Its meals include frogs, fish, and the eggs and chicks of ducks and other water birds. A snake's skin is thick and covered with tough scales.

The **water vole** is about the same size as a rat. It lives by the water, eating water plants and sometimes catching frogs and fish. It is a true vole, with a blunt nose, flat face, and small, furry ears. The vole's thick, dark brown fur keeps it warm. The fur also contains natural oils and waxes, making its coat glossy and waterproof. The vole grooms its coat with its paws and teeth. This helps to keep the coat clean and to spread the oils over the fur.

Is that a harmless log in the water? No, it's an **alligator**. It is ready to grab any prey in its wide mouth. After it has fed, the alligator may crawl out onto a dry bank to sunbathe. It can live in wet or dry places, as its scaly skin helps protect it from getting wet or drying out.

71

Eat each other?

Yes, almost certainly. Animals that hunt and eat other animals are called carnivores. They have long, sharp teeth. Some dinosaurs also had sharp, pointed teeth. They were probably carnivores, too. Like carnivores today, these meat-eating dinosaurs had different ways of hunting. Some chased their prey. Others hid, waiting to leap out on their victims. Some hunted alone. Others formed packs. Scavenging dinosaurs fed on the leftover scraps of dead animals.

Wolves hunt in packs. They can attack a large animal such as a caribou or elk. During the Age of Dinosaurs, **Velociraptor** (vel-o-si-rap-tor) may have done the same. Several may have formed a group to hunt a large dinosaur. They could bite with their sharp teeth and slash with their claws. Their prey had little defense against an attack like this.

Tarbosaurus (<u>tar</u>-bo-<u>saw</u>-rus), a huge meat-eater, was almost as tall as a house. It may have caught its prey by sprinting after it for a short time. Or perhaps Tarbosaurus arrived at a dead dinosaur killed by other animals, frightened the killers away, then ate its meal. Its teeth were bigger than your hands, and sharp enough to slice up flesh.

Dilophosaurus (dy-<u>lo</u>-fo-saw-rus) had long, thin, dagger-like teeth. They were ideal for jabbing at prey to kill it and for ripping off lumps of meat. Dilophosaurus also had long, slim legs. It may have been able to run twice as fast as you!

Some dinosaurs may have hunted mainly one kind of animal. **Baryonyx** (<u>bar</u>-ee-<u>on</u>-ix) had strong back legs for running, and a large thumb claw. Perhaps it waded through rivers and jabbed fish with its big claw, hooking them out of the water. Its mouth was like a crocodile's, long and narrow, and filled with small, sharp teeth. These teeth were suited to eating fish.

73

Live in the woods?

Yes, they do. In fact, more creatures live in woods and forests than anywhere else on Earth. Each type of natural place, such as a wood, a swamp, a grassland, a pond, a desert, or an ocean, is called a habitat. Wood and forest habitats are the world's richest places for wildlife. The trees provide many kinds of foods, such as leaves, shoots, fruits, and roots. They also give shelters, homes, and nests for thousands of kinds of insects, birds, mammals, and other animals.

The **hedgehog** could easily be called a "woodhog". This spiny, prickly relative of moles and shrews snuffles among the fallen leaves. It searches for slugs, snails, worms, grubs, and other small snacks. The average hedgehog has about 5,000 sharp spines. It rolls up into a ball to protect itself from foxes and other predators.

Beware of the **brown bear**, especially a mother with her cub. To protect her offspring, she charges and fights anyone who comes near. Brown bears live in forests and mountain areas in northwest North America, where they are sometimes called grizzlies. They also live in parts of Europe and across northern Asia. Brown bears eat almost any food, from leaves and fruits to insects, fish, and young deer.

74

Deer, such as the **white-tailed deer**, are well adapted to life in open woodland, where they graze on shoots and leaves. When in danger, they can hide in the thick undergrowth or race to safety among the tree trunks. As the deer runs, the bright flash of white fur beneath its tail acts as a warning to other members of the herd.

Have you heard a noise like a machine gun deep in the woods? It may be a **green woodpecker** "drumming" on a tree, with a series of very fast pecks. The woodpecker makes tiny holes with its long, sharp beak. It searches under the bark for beetles, grubs, and other small animals. Its skull and neck are very strong, so it does not get a headache!

The **gray wolf** was once common in woods across North America, Europe and Asia. However, many of these woods have been cut down for timber, firewood, and farmland. People were also afraid of wolves, and wolves sometimes attacked farm animals. Many wolves were hunted and killed. Now they are rare in many places, especially Europe. They have been driven from forests, up into mountains and out into deserts.

75

Have more than two eyes?

Not all bugs have more than two eyes. Most insects are "bug-eyed". They have two big eyes, one on each side of the head. People only have one lens in each eye, but insect "bug eyes" are made up of lots of tiny lenses. Some insects have extra eyes, which are smaller and simpler than the main ones. These "extra" eyes are often on top of the creature's head. Some spiders have only two eyes, while others have four, six, or even eight eyes. And there are also bugs that have no eyes at all. They live in caves, in the soil or in the water, where there is little or no light. Without light, eyes are useless!

This **zebra jumping spider** is looking at you! Its main pair of eyes are big and shiny. There are also three pairs of smaller eyes on the sides of its head. These can see things moving nearby, such as small insects. Once it has spotted the prey, the spider turns to face it and takes a good look with its main eyes. It judges how far away the victim is – and then jumps in for the kill.

Would you like eyes on stalks that wave around your head, and then pull back into your face for safety? The **giant African land snail** has an eye at the tip of each tentacle, which can do exactly this. But these eyes can't see details. They pick out only blurred patches of light and dark. That's enough for the snail to find its food. This fist-sized mollusk eats crops, dead animals, and even other snails.

The biggest eyes in the bug world belong to the **dragonfly**. Each eye has more than 5,000 separate lenses, like a tiny, bulging mosaic. Each lens sees only a small area. But the areas join together, like pieces of a jigsaw, to form a complete view. This fierce hunter can see a tiny midge as it flies in the dimness of dusk.

The **giant Australian earthworm** is no ordinary worm. It grows up to 13 feet (4 meters) long, is thicker than a thumb, and squirts a horrible-smelling liquid at its enemies! Proper eyes aren't much use in the darkness of the soil, so earthworms don't have them. But they do have light-detecting patches of skin, especially on the upper part of the head, to warn when they get too near the surface.

If you open your eyes underwater, things look blurred. Our eyes are designed for seeing in air. The **whirligig beetle** does not have that problem. This tiny beetle swims and whirls rapidly in circles on the surface of a pond. Each of its eyes is divided into two parts. The top half looks up into the air. The bottom half looks down into the water.

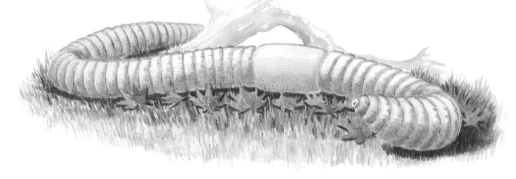

DO ANIMALS...
Have baths and showers?

You probably wash your face each morning and evening. Perhaps you have a bath or shower with soap or gel. This helps to get rid of dirt, dust, and body smells and cleans your hair, skin, and nails. Animals keep themselves clean, too. They may use water or mud, or their tongues, fingers, or claws. They may even get a friend to help.

The **housefly** paddles in dirt and muck and when it eats it licks up all kinds of disgusting things. But if you watch a fly you will probably see it rubbing its legs together and brushing its head or wings. Despite its filthy habits, it is a clean insect.

Elephants love to squirt water over themselves. This helps to keep them cool in the hot sun. They also like to bathe – in mud! The mud helps to get rid of flies and pests that irritate the elephant's skin. The mud also dries to form an extra "skin". This protects the elephant against sunburn and biting insects.

All cats keep themselves clean. They have very rough tongues, like sandpaper, to lick dirt and pests from their fur. This **leopard** is washing its face. It rubs one paw over its face to remove mud, leaves, and insects, then licks the paw to make it clean.

Like most birds, the **jay** combs and cleans its feathers with its beak. Sometimes lice and other pests get under the feathers and grab on to the bird's skin. So the jay gets some help. It squats in an ants' nest or holds ants in its beak. The ants nip the lice and pests from the jay's skin.

Most baby animals cannot wash themselves, so their mother usually does it for them. The mother **fox**, called a vixen, licks her cubs clean. The fox family lives in a large hole, called a den, until the cubs are several weeks old. The mother keeps the den clean, too. She carries droppings and old bedding outside in her mouth.

79

Use weapons?

Yes, they certainly did! They did not have guns or bombs, of course. But dinosaurs did have swords, spears, daggers, whips, and clubs, and these could be very dangerous. A dinosaur's weapons were parts of its body – its tail, teeth, horns, or claws. The meat-eating dinosaurs used their weapons to catch, kill, and cut up their prey. The plant-eating dinosaurs had weapons to defend themselves and fight back against the meat-eaters. They may also have used their weapons to battle against rivals for control of their herd, or to win mates at breeding time.

If **Pentaceratops** (pen-ta-serra-tops) lowered its head and charged, you would soon get out of the way. This dinosaur's name means "five-horned face". Most of the time, it probably grazed peacefully on plants. If threatened, Pentaceratops could have charged and jabbed enemies with its spear-like horns. It was three times the weight of today's rhinoceros.

In olden times, soldiers often carried huge clubs to war. **Euoplocephalus** (yoo-oh-plo-sef-al-us) had a club, too – on its tail. This dinosaur's tail ended in two heavy lumps of bone. When in danger, it may have turned around and swiped at its attacker with its tail.

Swift and silent, **Deinonychus** (dy-<u>non</u>-i-kus) may have raced up behind its prey. Leaping into the air, it probably kicked out with its feet and slashed at the prey with the long, curved claw on the second toe of each foot. When Deinonychus ran, it held these claws clear of the ground to keep them sharp.

Even if you had a dagger, would you attack a powerful creature such as an elephant? Probably not. **Allosaurus** (<u>al</u>-oh-<u>saw</u>-rus) might also have been wary of using its teeth and claws against the mighty bulk of **Diplodocus** (dip-<u>lod</u>-oh-kus). This dinosaur was three times heavier than an elephant! It would probably have lashed with its tail, jabbed with its thumb-spikes, and used its weight to crush Allosaurus.

In a modern army, the tanks and armored cars are well defended. So was the dinosaur **Edmontonia** (ed-mon-<u>toh</u>-nee-ah). It had spikes and shields on its back, longer spikes on its shoulders and sides, and thick plates of bone, like armor-plating. The only place that a predator might have hurt was its soft underbelly.

Have babysitters?

Like human parents, animal parents sometimes get very busy. They may have to leave their young for a while, to hunt for food or chase away enemies. When human parents go out, friends or relatives, such as aunts and uncles, may look after the children. Some animals do the same, but babysitting is not very common in the animal world. It mainly happens among creatures that live in large groups.

This tiny **robin** is feeding a big baby cuckoo. Of course, she is not its real mother. The mother cuckoo always lays her egg in the nest of another bird, then flies away. When the baby cuckoo hatches, it pushes the other bird's eggs from the nest. The robin thinks the cuckoo chick is hers. So she and her mate keep feeding it until the "baby" is many times bigger than they are!

Meerkats live in long, winding burrows in the grasslands of Africa. They eat all kinds of food, from insects, lizards, birds, and other small creatures to leaves, seeds, and fruits. In a large group of about 30 meerkats there will be several families. The adults take turns looking after one another's young, so parents can go and look for food or defend the burrows against enemies.

When baby birds hatch, the first thing they usually see is their real mother. They follow her everywhere. But sometimes eggs get mixed up. A hen may sit on a duck's eggs by mistake. When the **ducklings** hatch, they see the hen and think she is their mother. Soon they start to walk behind her in a line. The hen has become their new mother, even though she may not want to be!

Giraffes are the tallest animals in the world. With their long legs and long necks, they can reach leaves high up in the trees. When parent giraffes go off to find food, they may leave their young behind. These babies gather in a group, called a crèche. Sometimes "aunties" babysit for the young giraffes to make sure they don't get into trouble.

83

Go swimming?

Some dinosaurs probably went into the water to escape from enemies or to chase prey. They paddled, splashed, and may have swum. But no dinosaurs lived in the water all the time. Three of the creatures shown here, which spent their lives in water, lived at the same time as the dinosaurs. They were reptiles, like the dinosaurs. But they were not dinosaurs. They belonged to other groups of reptiles, which swam in ancient seas.

Plesiosaurs (<u>plez</u>-ce-oh-<u>sors</u>) were fat-bodied reptiles with long necks and short tails. They probably used their paddle-shaped legs to row through the water. There were many kinds of plesiosaur. The biggest grew to be 50 feet (15 meters) long. They fed mainly on fish and sea creatures. Some people believe that a mysterious monster lives in a lake called Loch Ness, in Scotland – and that it's a plesiosaur.

Mosasaurs (<u>mo</u>-za-<u>sors</u>) had huge mouths containing rows of sharp teeth. They were fast swimmers and hunted fish, squid, and curly-shelled ammonites. Ammonites, which were related to squid, have all died out. The biggest mosasaurs were 40 feet (12 meters) long. They were sea lizards, relatives of today's monitor lizards.

Ichthyosaurs (<u>ik</u>-thee-oh-<u>sors</u>) looked like dolphins, but they were reptiles not mammals. The shape of both dolphins and ichthyosaurs is ideally suited to fast swimming. An ichthyosaur moved by swishing its tail from side to side, and steered with its paddle-shaped legs. It probably fed mainly on fish. Like all the sea reptiles shown here, it had to come to the surface to breathe.

Megalosaurus (<u>meg</u>-a-lo-<u>saw</u>-rus) was a big meat-eating dinosaur. Like most wild animals today, dinosaurs could probably swim when they had to. But they did not spend a long time in the water, especially sea water. The salt in sea water could damage their scales and skin.

Cetiosaurus (<u>see</u>-tee-oh-<u>saw</u>-rus) may have paddled along the beach, but it would not have swum in the ocean unless its life was in danger. Some dinosaurs may have hunted along the beach, but it's unlikely they went into the water. Today, reptiles such as sea snakes and certain types of turtles live in the oceans.

85

Go to the doctor?

Animals sometimes get ill and hurt themselves, just as you do. But they can't go to a doctor or dentist, because there isn't one. Instead, animals have to look after themselves. They know by instinct what to do. They may eat or drink something that works like a kind of medicine or they may lick and clean a wound. Animals know that they should lie quietly and rest to help them get better. You probably know how hard it is to do this for more than a few minutes!

The main food of **butterflies** is the sweet, honey-like nectar in flowers. But these beautiful insects also need other substances, such as minerals and vitamins, to stay healthy. So from time to time, they sip at a pool of animal urine, which contains many minerals. Luckily for us, we can buy vitamin and mineral tablets from a store.

Even a small cut can be very dangerous for a **hippopotamus**. Hippos live in muddy rivers, so if a cut is not covered up and the water is dirty, the injury can become infected and never heal. To avoid this the hippo rolls in wet earth to cover and protect the wound. Its bandage is made of mud!

Macaws and other parrots are colorful, tropical birds. They eat leaves, fruits, nuts, and seeds. Some also feed on small animals, such as insects and worms. If they don't eat enough different foods, they become ill. Then macaws prescribe their own medicine. They fly to special, soft rocks that are full of minerals. There they scrape the rocks with their beaks and eat the mineral-rich rock dust.

Big fish sometimes get bits of food left in their mouths and blood-sucking pests become attached to their skin and scales. They can't go to a dentist or doctor. Small fish, called **cleaner wrasse**, nibble away the old food and pests for them. The wrasses even clean inside the fishes' mouths. The bigger fish could easily eat the cleaner wrasses, but they never do.

Dogs like to munch meat and crack bones, but if they start to feel sick they may eat grass. Then they are sick and this clears any bad or rotten food from their stomachs. The dog's wild cousin, the wolf, does exactly the same thing. When they feel ill, dogs and wolves know what to do by instinct. These are the feelings they are born with.

87

Clean up their homes?

Your parents probably do most of the cleaning at home. Animals know that they must clean out their nests and burrows, too. If they didn't, they would be deep in skin, feathers, or fur – not to mention fleas and piles of droppings! Many animals spend lots of time tidying their homes and removing rubbish. They have no vacuum cleaners or brushes. Instead, they use their feet, claws, and mouths.

Harvest mice live in a nest the size and shape of a tennis ball. It is made out of woven grass stems. The mother harvest mouse is always going in and out through the small entrance hole, carrying rubbish in her mouth. She is clearing out droppings and bits of leftover food that her babies have not eaten.

Badgers are well known as very clean animals. Every few days, they clear out their set. This is the name we give to their underground home of tunnels and rooms. The badgers pull out all the old leaves, grass, and moss, which they use for bedding. Then they collect clean, dry bedding and take it into the set.

Many birds use their beaks to flick bits of old food and droppings from their nests. A **blue tit** nest may be occupied by more than ten chicks, who sometimes leave bits of their caterpillar dinners. The blue tit parents give the nest a good cleaning several times each day.

In an ants' nest, each **ant** has a special job to do. Soldiers protect the nest, foragers collect food, and cleaners keep it clean and neat. The cleaners scurry through the corridors in the nest, gathering rubbish and throwing it out of the entrance. Sometimes they have to collect the bodies of dead and dying nest members, too.

All **cats**, big and small, are neat and clean. They would never lie down to sleep on lumpy stones or sharp twigs. They remove any pieces of rubbish from their favorite resting place before settling down for a catnap. After all, would you sleep in a bed full of stones or sticks?

89

WHY DON'T PEOPLE
Like bugs?

People do like some bugs – most people think ladybugs are cute. But many insects and other creepy crawlies send shivers down our spines. Sometimes there's no good reason, because the creature is harmless. With others, though, we have good reason to fear. Some are pests, causing harm or damage. Others might bite, sting, or poison us. Some bugs spread germs, or illness. Others ruin our crops, plants, and food. Bugs can also cause diseases in our animals. They burrow into wood and other substances in our houses, buildings and other structures. They even eat our clothes!

The dreaded **Colorado beetle** can destroy huge fields of potatoes in a few days. Not on its own, of course, but in large numbers. It is easy to recognize. The beetle has yellow-and-black stripes and the larva is orange-red in color. Both eat potato-plant leaves. If you see them, tell the farmer at once. Pesticide sprays can kill them and will avoid a severe outbreak.

Aaargh, help! It's a **tarantula**! Many people flee in fear. Others keep spiders as pets. Various big, hairy spiders are called tarantulas. But some have other, proper names, such as bird-eating spider. Tarantulas can give a powerful and painful bite, but they rarely kill people. Small spiders, such as the black widow of North America and the redback of Australia, are far more dangerous.

Every few years, huge swarms of **locusts** build up in areas of Africa and Asia. They fly long distances to find food. If they land on fields of farm crops, they can eat vast amounts in a day. Then they move on, breeding as they go. It's a disaster on a massive scale. Thousands of people go hungry or even starve. The young locust nymphs are called hoppers because their wings are small and they cannot fly. One way to kill locusts is by spraying pesticides from aircraft.

Some bugs cause harm by spreading deadly diseases. In Africa, the **tsetse fly** spreads a disease called nagana, or sleeping sickness. The fly bites an animal or a human – an ox, perhaps, which has the disease. It takes in the germs as it sucks up the blood. When the fly bites its next victim, it "injects" the germs.

What has made the small holes in these gloves? It's the pesky **clothes moth**! Well, not the moth itself, but its caterpillars. The caterpillars change into pupae and then into adult moths, which lay eggs on the clothes again – it's a never-ending circle!

91

DO ANIMALS...
Like living with people?

Some do, such as our cats, dogs, and other pets. Also, some wild creatures have learned to depend on people. They live in and around our houses, stores, factories, and other buildings. They come into our gardens and parks. They share our food, sometimes whether we like it or not! These familiar animals may become so common that they are pests. We try to get rid of them, but they are very wary and difficult to catch. They keep well away from people. These creatures do not like us, but they do like the food, shelter, and surroundings that humans provide.

Wherever there are people, there are rats and mice. The **black rat**, or ship rat, is very common in warmer areas. It comes out at night, and it can easily climb up walls and ropes. It gnaws its way into food stores and leaves its droppings and urine, which spoil the food. The black rat also carries pests, such as fleas, and spreads diseases.

The **gray squirrel** is a common sight in gardens, parks, and woods, even in the middle of cities. It often comes to feed at bird tables. It looks cute and cuddly, but the gray squirrel has sharp teeth and claws, and it can bite and scratch hard. It damages trees and bushes by gnawing their bark.

The **Moorish gecko** is a type of lizard found in Mediterranean and Adriatic countries, and North Africa. It can climb well and clings to walls, windows, and doors with its sucker-like toes. Several kinds of geckoes come into houses and walk across the walls and ceilings, especially at night. They cause no harm. They even help by eating flies.

Before there were houses, **house martins** made their mud nests on steep cliffs and rocky outcrops. But a house wall does just as well. The martin clings to the wall with its small, sharp claws. The house's overhanging roof protects the bird and its cup-shaped nest from the rain. House martins eat small insects, which they catch in flight. Martins also make loud twittering noises, especially early in the morning!

Around the world, people try to get rid of **cockroaches** by using poisons, sprays, and traps. But these insects are great survivors and they are very difficult to kill. They get into houses, kitchens, food stores, factories, and other warm buildings. They come out at night and feed on almost anything, even paper and leather.

93

Index